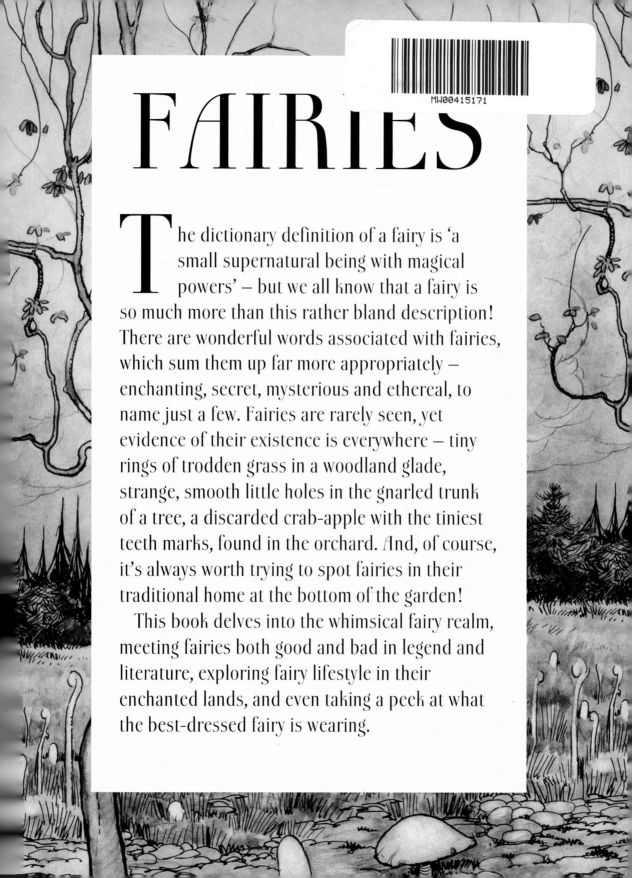

FAIRIES

T he dictionary definition of a fairy is 'a small supernatural being with magical powers' – but we all know that a fairy is so much more than this rather bland description! There are wonderful words associated with fairies, which sum them up far more appropriately – enchanting, secret, mysterious and ethereal, to name just a few. Fairies are rarely seen, yet evidence of their existence is everywhere – tiny rings of trodden grass in a woodland glade, strange, smooth little holes in the gnarled trunk of a tree, a discarded crab-apple with the tiniest teeth marks, found in the orchard. And, of course, it's always worth trying to spot fairies in their traditional home at the bottom of the garden!

This book delves into the whimsical fairy realm, meeting fairies both good and bad in legend and literature, exploring fairy lifestyle in their enchanted lands, and even taking a peek at what the best-dressed fairy is wearing.

A Fairy History

Some of the most often asked questions about fairies are: 'What is a fairy?', 'How long have fairies been in existence?', and – most importantly – 'Are fairies still to be seen?'

The answer is that fairies have lived in countries all around the world for centuries and, like mankind, have evolved. Today we think of fairies as pretty, winged creatures with a very kind, fun-loving nature, living in mounds and woodlands and in the gardens of those humans who have the good sense to believe in them. However, not all fairies are pretty and not all fairies are good, as we will discover when we meet the family of fairy folk – so how did they acquire this image?

In Britain, fairies have been around since Celtic times, and fairy forms, both good and evil, were very much a part of Celtic folklore. Even after many Celtic beliefs were banished as 'pagan' with the coming of Christianity, people still believed in fairies – indeed, they enjoyed quite a high profile in the romantic Elizabethan era, appearing in plays and poems. But it was the sentimental Victorians who really gave fairies their everlasting place in society. Beautiful fairies began to appear in paintings, on greetings cards, on packaging and in advertising campaigns. They appeared in stories and poetry. And they appeared in photographs – or did they? In 1917, two cousins in Yorkshire claimed to have taken pictures of fairies, and it wasn't until many years later that the two women admitted that the

LEFT: 'The sentimental Elf and the wayward Fairy', from Richard Doyle's 1875 publication, 'In Fairyland. A Series of Pictures from the Elf-World'. Regrettably, this charming liaison ended in tears when the fairy flounced off, leaving a heartbroken elf!

photographs were fake. Of course, they would be – after all, one can't photograph something that is not really of this world!

It is said that there are no fairies now, that they are all dead. But if you don't have faith in something, and believe in it wholeheartedly, it's not visible to you. If you do believe, however, just remember always to keep an eye open – you may be lucky!

RIGHT: The Victorian artist Sophie Anderson illustrates how a fairy is made: 'Take the fair face of woman, and gently suspending, with butterflies, flowers, and jewels attending, thus your fairy is made of most beautiful things.'

THE CHRISTMAS FAIRY

The lovely tradition of putting up a decorated tree at Christmas, with a doll dressed as a fairy on top, began in Victorian times. Originally the doll was meant to represent Jesus, but over time it was replaced by an angel or a fairy. Fairies are sometimes said to be angels in the making, if they're good – or 'fallen' angels, if they're naughty. The Christmas-tree fairy is without doubt the good kind!

Cicely Mary Barker's Christmas Tree Fairy.

Fairy Folk

We tend to think of fairies as beautiful, delicate creatures with benevolent natures.

We have visions of them bringing help and solace to humans who are sad, lonely or in trouble. But even the most appealing fairies can actually be quite naughty, and some little fairies are really not things of beauty at all – the fairy world includes goblins, gnomes and dwarfs. Of course, this does not necessarily make them bad, but dwarfs can be hostile towards humans, and goblins, regrettably, are generally very bad indeed.

BROWNIES

Small and very secretive, brownies are to be found in Scotland and the north of England, and are very useful fairies to have in the home or around a farm. So-named because they have brown skin and wear brown clothes, these helpful, shaggy, practical little creatures will creep out at night to help with the housework and do odd jobs in the garden or farmyard. Brownies are very loyal, attaching themselves to a household, and it is worth looking out for them as they can very occasionally be seen – but only when they want to be.

ELVES

There are two types of elves – light and dark. Both have formidable magical powers, but whereas light elves – who live above ground –

FAIRIES IN HUMAN FORM

F airy words are often used to describe humans, which makes one wonder whether those humans are actually fairies … the word 'elfin', for example, is used to describe a diminutive, delicate person, particularly one possessed of an unusual charm. And have you ever noticed someone with 'pixie' features? Look out for that telltale turned-up nose, and for ears that are rather suspiciously pointed at the top …

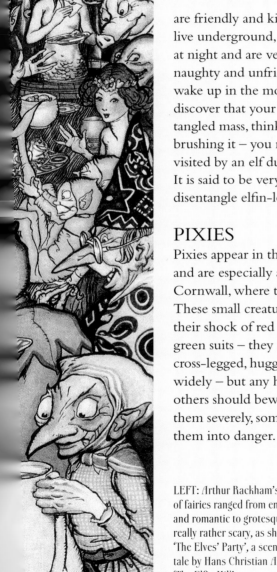

are friendly and kindly, dark elves live underground, only come out at night and are very definitely naughty and unfriendly. If you wake up in the morning and discover that your hair is in a tangled mass, think twice before brushing it – you may have been visited by an elf during the night. It is said to be very unlucky to disentangle elfin-locks!

PIXIES

Pixies appear in the West Country, and are especially associated with Cornwall, where they are known as 'piskies'. These small creatures look very appealing with their shock of red hair, turned-up noses and green suits – they are often portrayed sitting cross-legged, hugging their knees and grinning widely – but any human who is unkind to others should beware, as pixies will punish them severely, sometimes even leading them into danger.

ABOVE: Pixies are known to punish unwise humans. Here, the pixie has a decided air of disapproval as he watches a human enjoying his pipe, so perhaps he was an early advocate of the anti-smoking campaign!

LEFT: Arthur Rackham's portrayal of fairies ranged from endearing and romantic to grotesque and really rather scary, as shown in 'The Elves' Party', a scene from a tale by Hans Christian Andersen, 'The Elfin Hill'.

GOBLINS

Goblins – also known as hobgoblins and sometimes sprites – are grotesque little creatures who follow a nomadic lifestyle, living for short periods in caves or in woodlands, hiding in hollows in the roots of ancient trees, but quickly moving on. Goblins are extremely mischievous, which is possibly why they never stay in one place for long – they love hiding things or changing signs around to confuse humans, so a hasty retreat is probably wise!

DWARFS

Dwarfs are small, with very long beards. They live underground in caves or holes and are known to be very industrious, digging in mines for gems and precious metals which they make into extraordinarily beautiful jewellery and tools – they are renowned for their metal-working skills.

Their puny stature has led to their name being used as a verb – to 'dwarf' something means that an unusually large object or person makes any smaller object or person seem comparatively very small indeed!

RIGHT: This jolly fellow is Charles Folkard's 1911 depiction of Robin Goodfellow, or Puck, a sprite who played tricks on humans. If Robin/Puck led you astray, turning your cloak inside out helped you find your way again.

LEFT: These wicked little goblins are doing what they love best – confounding humans!

GNOMES

Gnomes live below ground to guard the treasures of the earth. These small, misshapen creatures are unsociable and avoid contact with humans. If they are exposed to sunlight they immediately turn to stone, yet many seem to have made this mistake and not

ALWAYS RESPECT FAIRIES

Fairies are sensitive creatures, and if you are thoughtless it is very easy to offend them. Always remember to leave a gift to say 'thank you' to a helpful fairy – a wisp of fine fabric for a new dress, perhaps, or a thimble-ful of creamy milk or a glossy, ripe black-berry. However, never offer a suit of clothes to a brownie as this would immediately break the bond between you and your helpful housekeeper could well depart in a huff. Even good fairies can become extremely naughty if you upset them.

Tricks that might be played on the careless culprit include:

- pulling the covers off your bed while you are asleep
- leaving gates open to let animals escape
- stuffing birds' nests into chimneys so that the house fills with smoke.

regretted it, as stone gnomes often appear in groups in humans' gardens, transformed into plump, cheerful, amusing fellows who spend their time carrying out all manner of useful tasks such as fishing, digging and weeding!

RIGHT: Although by nature gnomes like to keep themselves to themselves, humans have interpreted their characters as friendly and helpful. Indeed, collecting stone gnomes to decorate the garden has become a fascinat-ing hobby for many humans.

ABOVE: In Arthur Rackham's 1905 watercolour 'The Changeling', the fairy folk appear to be taking very good care of the human baby they have stolen, even providing a musical welcome with a miniature marching band.

Fairies and Children

While fairies, both good and bad, can appear to humans of any age, they seem to have a very special affinity with children.

Perhaps this is because children are more inclined to believe in them; or it may be that fairies simply find children more fun to be with, as their imaginations are still free and unfettered – not yet weighed down by solemn, grown-up inhibitions.

As long as they are polite and considerate, children may be allowed to watch fairies dancing or playing, or to listen to their fairy music. Rude children should beware, however – fairies will often take it upon themselves to correct their behaviour, which is helpful for other people, but can be rather unpleasant for the child in question!

While children may be fascinated by fairies, fairies can also be fascinated by children. A fairy will sometimes steal a human child and leave a fairy child – a changeling – in its place in the hope that the parents will not notice. This seems like something that would only have happened in days long gone, but every now and again you might come across a strangely magical child who doesn't seem to quite fit its family, and wonder – just fleetingly – if a fairy has been at work …

ABOVE: Children pit their strength against the fairies in a tussle with a giant snowball. From the perturbed expressions on the children's faces – very rosy from their efforts – it seems that the fairies are winning!

PETER PAN

The most renowned literary fairy is Tinker Bell in J.M. Barrie's classic story, *Peter Pan*. This wonderful fantasy, about three children and their adventures in the Neverland, reveals the method for keeping fairies alive – which is for all children who believe in fairies to clap their hands like mad! *Peter Pan* has come to represent the special bond between fairies and children, as all proceeds from the sales of the book are donated to the famous London children's hospital, Great Ormond Street.

Mabel Lucie Attwell's Peter Pan.

Fairyland

Where do fairies live? The answer is that, with a few exceptions, they live outdoors, using the treasures of the natural world to create perfect homes in miniature.

ABOVE: Fairies are very resourceful when it comes to interior design – in this illustration for J.M. Barrie's 'Peter Pan', they are weaving curtains from leaves for their underground home.

Wherever you look in the country-side, there will be evidence of fairies – tiny rings made by dancing fairies, little hollows in the gnarled old trunks of trees, grassy glades in bluebell woods and magical fairy mounds.

Those plump little hummocks that dot the fields and woodlands, covered in a layer of deliciously soft moss, may well hide an exquis-ite fairy home. Imagine the scene inside – a dome-shaped cavern, filled with the light of a hundred glow-worms. The walls are lined with the velvety, fragrant petals of dog roses in the most delicate shade of pink, while the earthy floor is covered in a patchwork

carpet of pale-green nasturtium leaves, sewn together with minute fairy stitches. In the centre of the hall stands the table – a large, round, red toadstool spotted with white, surrounded by a circle of tiny toadstools for the fairies to sit on. Acorn cups filled with clover honey and jellies made from blackberries, crab-apples and rose-hips stand on

THE DUNVEGAN FAIRY FLAG

On the romantic Scottish Isle of Skye stands Dunvegan Castle, the sturdy stronghold of the ancient Clan MacLeod. This castle has a curious treasure – a faded, tattered old flag. But, according to legend, the threadbare flag once belonged to the fairy wife of one of the first MacLeod chiefs, and has magical powers. Should the MacLeods be in danger, they can unfurl the fairy flag, wave it three times, and they will be safe. However, the magic will only work three times, and it has been used twice already.

ABOVE: 'Come, now a roundel!' cries Titania, queen of the fairies, in Shakespeare's 'A Midsummer Night's Dream'. A ring of tiny mushrooms, as shown here, is always evidence that fairies have been about.

BELOW: The fly agaric – a red and white spot-ted mushroom – is often associated with fairies. In this delightful 1927 illustration by Mildred Entwisle, it makes a very decorative frame for a merry-go-round.

wooden shelves. Set around the walls are the fairy beds, with deep, downy mattresses made from the silky fluff of old man's beard, plucked from the wild clematis in the hedgerow when the flowers have gone to seed.

Fairies love to party, and music-making and dancing are among their favourite pastimes. They often join hands and dance in circles, leaving behind them fairy rings of dark green grass; or they might dance around the maypole, or a fairy tree such as the oak or hawthorn. If you are very quiet, it is possible to hear them and even see them – but you must be careful not to let them see you.

Fairy Tales

Fairy tales are written for children and carry a wise message,
usually demonstrating the triumph of good over evil.

But while fairy tales always involve an element of magic, they don't always appear to feature fairies! This is because fairies often appear in mysterious guises to test aspects of human character, such as loyalty or integrity. Once the hero or heroine has shown that he or she possesses the quality under scrutiny, or has learned the lesson the fairy is trying to teach, the fairy reveals its true form.

ABOVE: Beneath a starlit sky, a gloriously stately Titania, attended by her fairies and elves, meets Oberon, the handsome king of the fairies, with his goblin pageboys, in Shakespeare's 'A Midsummer Night's Dream'.

Fairies do not only appear in children's stories, however – sometimes they feature in classical literature and music, too. One of Shakespeare's great plays is *A Midsummer Night's Dream*. Midsummer is a very magical time for

LEFT: 'The Queen of the Fairies appears to Prince Arthur' in this painting by Henry Fuseli for Edmund Spenser's 'The Faerie Queene'. Prince Arthur was the older brother of King Henry VIII, portrayed in the poem as Oberon.

everyone, but especially so for fairies, for this is when they come out to celebrate. The stars of this piece are Oberon, whom Shakespeare portrays as the king of the fairies, and Titania, his queen, who together rule their fairy court. Oberon also appears in a poem by Edmund Spenser, an Elizabethan poet, called *The Faerie Queene*. Here, Oberon is portrayed as the father of Spenser's fairy queen, whom he calls Gloriana – the name given to Elizabeth I to honour the success of her reign.

Fairy stories such as *The Sleeping Beauty* and *Cinderella* have been set to music and choreographed as ballets; but perhaps the most enchanting marriage of fairy music and dance is the wonderful *Nutcracker Suite*. Here, a young girl (who has possibly indulged in rather too much rich food at her family's Christmas party!) dreams of gifts and edible treats coming to life, such as in the delightful 'Dance of the Sugar Plum Fairy'.

ABOVE: This illustration for the enchanting ballet 'The Nutcracker', written by the Russian composer Tchaikovsky in 1892, was painted by Ida Rintoul Outhwaite. It appeared on the front cover of a 1941 publication of the sheet music.

THE WATER BABIES

A small boy – a chimney sweep – runs away from his wicked master and is turned into a water baby by the fairies. But, like many people who have been treated unkindly, Tom is himself unkind. He learns his lesson from a fairy who appears in two forms – Mrs Be-done-by-as-you-did, an ugly and stern old woman who metes out just punishment for Tom's naughtiness, and Mrs Do-as-you-would-be-done-by, a plump and warm and loving girl who shows Tom how much better it is to be kind.

ABOVE: Snow White's vain stepmother was outraged when her mirror told her: 'Snow White is the fairest of them all.' Here, Snow White lights candles for the seven dwarfs who shelter her from her stepmother's evil intentions.

CINDERELLA

Cinderella's wicked stepmother and stepsisters make her do chores instead of attending a ball thrown by a highly eligible prince. But Cinderella's fairy godmother transforms her rags into an elegant gown with dainty glass slippers. Cinderella goes to the ball, with a warning to be home by midnight, when the magic will end. Unfortunately Cinderella leaves it a little late, and loses a slipper in her haste to flee; but the prince has fallen in love with her, and scours the country to find the foot that fits the slipper. The outcome is a happy marriage for Cinderella and her prince, and two very dejected wicked stepsisters – a classic tale of good overcoming evil.

THE SLEEPING BEAUTY

A king and queen throw a wonderful christening party for their baby daughter. Six good fairies attend and bestow warm and loving

SNOW WHITE AND THE SEVEN DWARFS

Snow White is so beautiful that her jealous stepmother orders a huntsman to kill her. Instead he leaves her deep in the forest, where seven benevolent dwarfs look after her. But the stepmother discovers Snow White's whereabouts and determines to kill her. She almost succeeds, with a poisoned apple, but then a handsome prince falls in love with Snow White, and when the dwarfs pick up her glass coffin to carry her to the prince's palace, the apple is dislodged, and the princess revives. The shock kills Snow White's stepmother – a rather extreme lesson that being envious gets you nowhere!

RIGHT: In this 1894 painting by William Robert Symonds of The Princess and The Frog, the frog retrieves the princess's golden ball and looks hopeful of receiving his reward – a kiss. The princess, however, looks less enthusiastic!

ABOVE: An offended fairy (who was carelessly left off the christening guest list) casts a spell on the princess who, on her 16th birthday, will fall asleep for a hundred years – the Sleeping Beauty.

wishes upon the child, but the joy of the occasion is ruined when a wicked fairy – whom the king and queen have forgotten to invite – casts an evil spell on the baby. When the girl turns 16, she pricks her finger on a spinning wheel, and the evil spell manifests. She falls asleep for a hundred years, until her prince finds her and awakens her with a kiss. This is another tale about good overcoming evil, but also teaches that people who feel hurt tend to retaliate.

THE PRINCESS AND THE FROG

A kind and handsome prince is turned into an ugly frog by a witch and doomed to live in a pond until he is kissed by a princess. One day a princess comes along, and accidentally drops her golden ball into the pond. The frog offers to retrieve it for her if she will kiss him. The idea really doesn't appeal to her, but eventually she agrees and plants a kiss on the frog's mouth. He immediately turns back into a prince, and the couple fall in love. The princess's lesson is that things aren't always as they appear, and what is ugly on the outside may be beautiful within. Of course, the opposite is also true!

FAIRY GODMOTHERS

Rather like a guardian angel, a fairy godmother is a very desirable thing to have. These benevolent beings, full of love and sympathy, appear to those who are in need of some kindess, and – with a quick wave of a magic wand – change their unhappy pasts into rosy futures. Of course, the magic itself can be short-lived – Cinderella had to keep a very close eye on the clock – but once the transformation has begun, the rest usually unfolds smoothly.

Cinderella sets off for the ball in her carriage, magicked from a humble pumpkin. Her fairy godmother – who looks rather alarming, but also very kindly – warns Cinderella to leave on the stroke of midnight.

The Cowslip Fairy

Flower Fairies™

Shortly after the end of the First World War, a delightful new breed of fairies appeared – the Flower Fairies™.

These endearing little creatures were painted by one Cicely Mary Barker, and the first 'collection', *Flower Fairies of the Spring*, published in 1923, was an instant success. *Flower Fairies of the Summer*, *Autumn* and *Winter* soon followed, along with *Flower Fairies of the Garden*, *Flower Fairies of the Trees*, *Flower Fairies of the Wayside*, *A Flower Fairy Alphabet*, and a number of short stories.

Cicely took her inspiration from a belief in 'truth to nature', and this is reflected in her portrayal in fairy form of a glorious array of trees, flowers and even those unfortunate plants that have come to be referred to as 'weeds'. A quick glance at a flower fairy picture shows an adorable fairy character – girl or boy – wearing a pretty dress or a neat little suit, but closer inspection reveals a quite extraordinary attention to detail, worthy of the most careful botanical record. Every leaf, every petal, every berry, every butterfly wing is perfect – you can almost smell the lavender, taste the cherries and feel the prickles of the horse-chestnut casing that one brave boy fairy wears as a hat. The fairies were modelled on the 'real' children

LEFT: The Bluebell Fairy looks very proud, which is quite justified as fairy spells and enchantments are woven in bluebell woods. Fairies are summoned to their moonlit jaunts by the ringing of a bluebell.

BLODEUWEDD – THE ORIGINAL FLOWER FAIRY

BELOW: An acorn cup (such a useful item in the fairy world) makes a very striking cap for a little boy fairy, and perhaps inspires him to be 'strong and good', like the wood of the oak tree.

Blodeuwedd – 'Flower Face' – was created from flowers as a beautiful bride for Llew Llaw Gyffes, the sun god. All was well until Blodeuwedd fell in love with another man and conspired to kill her husband, who eventually defeated his rival in battle. As Blodeuwedd fled through the night skies, she left a trail of white flowers behind her, which became a galaxy of stars – the Milky Way. Blodeuwedd's story seems a tragic one, but is actually symbolic of creation, blossoming and death as the seasons change through the year, a familiar theme in Celtic lore.

E. Wallcousins' illustration of Blodeuwedd greeting her lover.

who attended Cicely's sister's school, dressed in wonderful fairy costumes with wings made from twigs and gauze.

Each flower fairy is accompanied by an educational poem that describes the nature of the plant, or what it is especially well known for. The May, for example, says 'And lo, where I am come indeed, / The Spring and Summer meet', a reference to the pagan Beltane festival on 1 May, when cattle were driven to their summer pastures. Traditionally, crowns of hawthorn blossom were worn on May Day. Of the less welcome Sow Thistle, it is said 'They think me a tiresome fellow—/An ugly weed/And a rogue indeed; …'. Cicely also adds fascinating facts as asides, such as: 'Country people make wine from them [elderberries]; and boys make whistles from elder stems.'

Fairy Fashions

Some fairies are really not too bothered about their attire – goblins and dwarfs, for example, go for the workmanlike, rather than the sartorial, approach.

ABOVE: The soft, delicate colours of sweet peas are perfect for little girls. Here, a fairy child tries a new bonnet on her baby sister and declares: 'I really think/Nothing's more becoming/Than this pretty pink!'

But for those delicate fairies who strongly resemble real boys and girls on a minute scale, the opportunities for looking their best are unlimited. And because much of what they wear comes from the natural world, they can change their outfits with the seasons, choosing fresh, silvery-green leaves and pastel blossoms in the spring, brightly coloured blooms all through the summer, and then all the wonderful shades of autumn leaves until spring rolls round again. Of course, if you were careless enough to leave lying about a tiny swatch of whisper-soft lawn in an irresistibly pretty colour, a girl fairy could be forgiven for stealing it away and transforming it into a gorgeous new gown for a very special occasion …

Fairies love to wear hats! Some flowers simply beg to be worn on the head – snowdrops, blue-bells and sweet peas for the dainty, demure look; daffodils and foxgloves for a rather more stylish touch; and vibrant orange marigolds to make a splash at a celebration. For simplicity, though, there is nothing to beat a little daisy chain, worn as a crown – and making one is such an

absorbing pastime for a fairy on a lazy summer afternoon. Boy fairies also have a great sense of fun when it comes to hats – a pine cone is a witty addition to a midwinter outfit, while an elm leaf, stitched into a cone shape, looks particularly well with an elf's green suit.

As for wings – well, suffice to say that butterflies and moths come in all sorts of sizes and colours, and make very obliging accessories for fairies. And remember to keep a watchful eye out for the deliciously fine gossamer that floats on the air when a light breeze is blowing – harnessed into wing shape, it goes with anything and is ideal for lending lightness to flight.

ABOVE: This chic fairy, painted in 1914 by M.T. Ross, shows how a variety of autumn leaves and berries can be used to add a striking finishing touch to a simple fitted dress.

Fairy Food

Fairies who work hard enjoy a little solid sustenance – perhaps a bowl of nourishing soup or porridge, or, in the case of Brownies who can be so helpful with the household chores, some delicious fresh cream.

ABOVE: These children seem rather surprised to come across a fairy market, with bowls of fresh fruit and berries for sale, and fabrics and pots – but where else would a fairy go for all these necessities of life?

ABOVE: Apples are closely associated with the West Country. Here, fairies and elves are shown picking apples in an illustration for Eden Phillpotts' book 'A Dish of Apples', set in Devonshire.

Mostly, though, fairies eat a light but healthy diet of foods to be found in the countryside. They are particularly fond of apples and blackberries, both of which are recognized in country folklore as being associated with fairies – the small, immature apples that cling to the tree at the end of the season are known as 'the pixie harvest', while in some areas it is considered taboo to eat blackberries as they are known to be the exclusive property of the fairy folk.

Like bees, fairies feed on nectar from flow-ers and love to share the honey that the bees make. They are also very partial to milk, and

Helen Jacobs.

Acknowledgements

Text by Jenni Davis. The author has asserted her moral rights.
Edited by Jenni Davis.
Picture research by Jan Kean and Jenni Davis.
Designed by Nick Avery.

Photographs are reproduced by kind permission of the following:
AKG: 13 top left, 14 top; Bridgeman Art Library: fc, ifc/1, 2/3 above,
4 top right, 6 left, 8, 9 below, 10 top, 12 below, 13 below right,
14 below, 15 above, 20 above left, 20/21 top, CD; Fortean Picture
Library: 2 below left, 5 right (above and below), 11 above, 12 top,
19 right; Mary Evans Picture Library: 4 above, 4/5, 6 top right, 7 left,
9 above, 10 below, 10/11, 13 top right, 15 below, 17 below, 18 above
left, 20 below left; Rex Features: 7 right, bc.
Flower Fairies™ illustrations (3 below, 16, 17 right, 18 top right, 18/19)
and poems by Cicely Mary Barker, copyright © The Estate of Cicely
Mary Barker, 1923, 1926, 1940, 1944, 1948, 1990. Reproduced by
permission of Frederick Warne & Co.

Publication in this form © Jarrold Publishing 2004, latest reprint 2006.
No part of this publication may be reproduced by any means without
the permission of Jarrold Publishing and the copyright holders.

Pitkin Guides is an imprint of Jarrold Publishing, Norwich.

Printed in Singapore.
ISBN-13: 978-1-84165-135-4
ISBN-10: 1-84165-135-4   2/06

FRONT COVER: 'Fairy with Wings', a gloriously whimsical
portrayal by Charles Folkard.

BACK COVER: Fairies at the Serpentine, an illustration by
Arthur Rackham from 'Peter Pan'.

are not above helping themselves when they
come across an unattended cow in a pasture or
barn. They often keep herds of 'fairy' cattle, a
very useful breed that provide an endless supply
of milk. In Celtic lore, the cow was a symbol of
nourishment, love and protection, and was one
of the sacred animals of Brighid, the Celtic
goddess of inspiration, healing, crafts and fertil-
ity. Brighid was raised on the milk of fairy
cattle, and had a special herd of her own.

   Human children love those special little
cakes that are called 'fairy cakes' because they
are so sweet and light and delicate – just like
good fairies in stories. Topped with a drift of
icing and a sprinkle of hundreds and thousands
in bright colours, fairy cakes are often served at
birthday parties, where a touch of very special
fairy magic is called upon – to make the birthday wish come true.

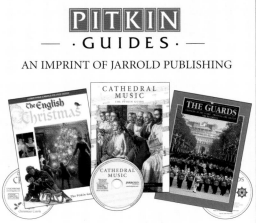

PITKIN

ISBN 1-84165-135-4

9 781841 651354